Wedding

Lynne Hannigan
Photographs by Ed Barber

A&C Black · London

My name is Angela and this is my class at Ripple
Infants' School. Today I've got some exciting
news. I'm going to be a bridesmaid for the first
time in my life! The bride is my granny's friend,
Lydia, and the groom is called William.

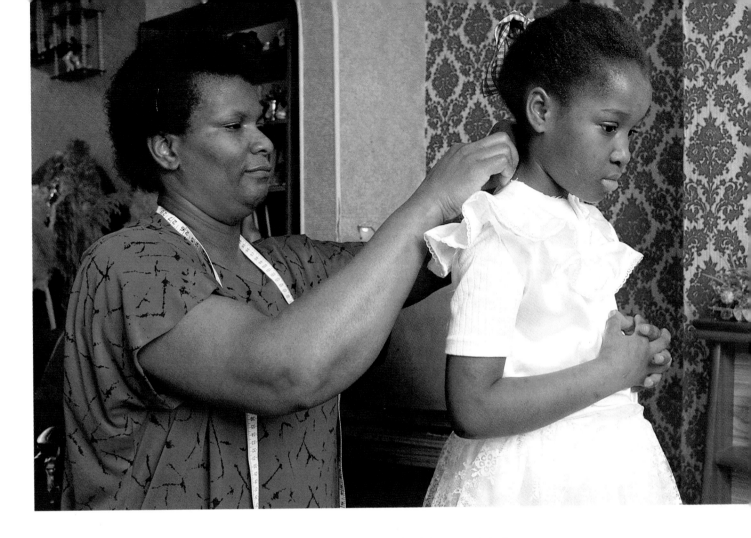

Lydia's mum is making all the bridesmaids'
dresses and, after school, I go to try mine on.

I haven't been to Lydia's house before, so I keep
quiet. Lydia's mum pins my dress together and I try
it on carefully so that the pins don't stick into me.

The dress is white with
lace all over it.
'Do you think pink would
be prettier?' says
Lydia's mum.

I stand very still while
she makes the dress fit. I
wonder if Princess Diana
feels like this when she
tries on her new
dresses.

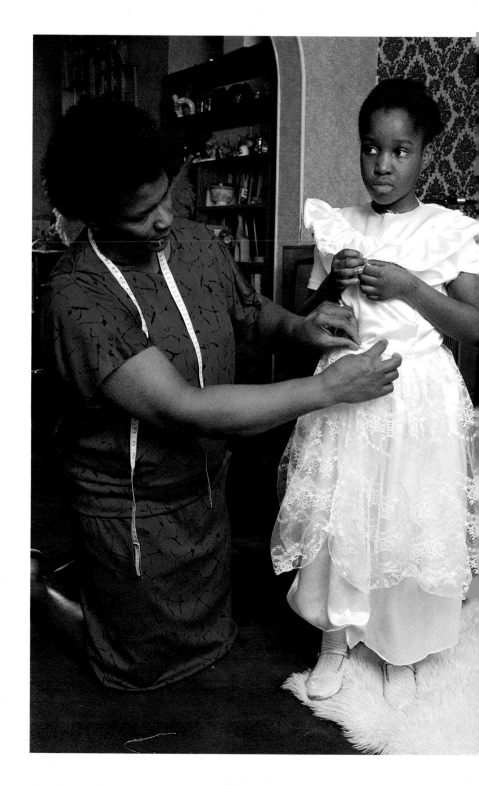

Lydia and her sister Caroline are making our head-dresses out of wire and pearls. They can't decide what looks best.

'Shall we have one row of pearls or two?'
We all start laughing because Caroline keeps pulling faces.

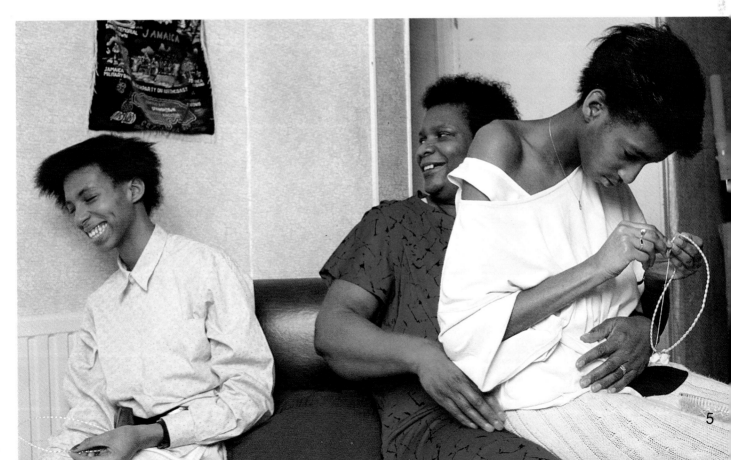

At school, we decide to find out
some more about weddings.
Everyone tries to bring in old
wedding clothes, or pictures.

We start making a picture of a
bride in a white wedding dress.
It's supposed to be Lydia, but the
face goes a bit wrong.

To make her dress, we screw up
lots of pieces of tissue and stick
them on to a big piece of paper.

a Hindu bridegroom

a Hindu bride

a Muslim bridegroom

a Muslim bride

Then we make pictures of some different clothes
which people wear when they get married.

Jodie thinks it's a good idea for the men to have
nice clothes to dress up in.

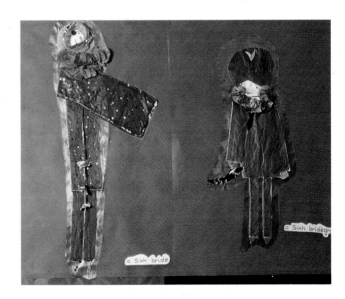

a Sikh bride

a Sikh bridegroom

There's a lot to do, so my grandma says she'll come and help us. Grandma is a nurse, and today is her day off.

She helps Alison and Roy to make garlands. The bridegroom at an Asian wedding wears beautiful garlands of flowers like these.

Mrs De Zoysa had a Hindu wedding. She says when she was married, her sisters decorated her hands with mendhi. She shows us how to make mendhi patterns from henna mixed with water.

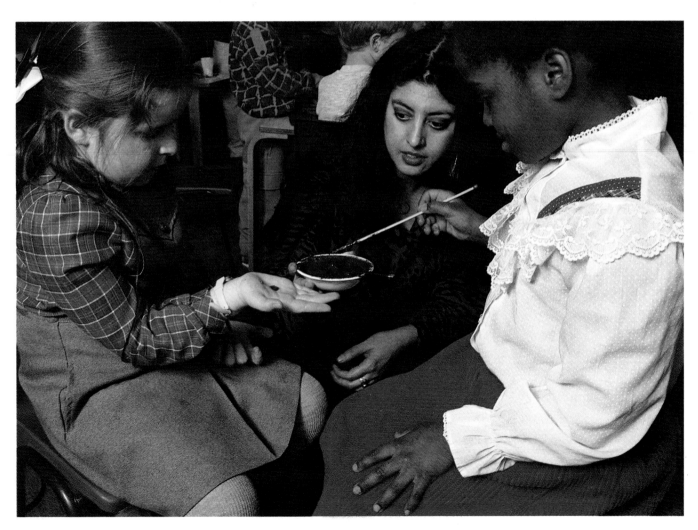

On Saturday, Lydia and Caroline go to choose the flowers for the wedding.

I'm going to carry a basket with pink and white flowers. I'll have a head-dress to match and I'll wear a pink dress instead of a white one.
The older bridesmaids will carry posies.

At school, some of us are making posies out of paper. We put drops of perfume on the posies to make them smell nice.

William's mum and his sister Joycelyn have made some cakes for the wedding.

Two of them are very special. One is from William to Lydia and one is from Lydia to William. They have words of love written on them.

At school, we are tasting some wedding food from different countries. There's ladoo and jelaybies as well as wedding cake.

We make our favourite foods out of cardboard and stick them on to paper plates. Our teacher, Mr Pocock, says that Gurjit's samosas look good enough to eat.

This week, Mr Pocock is taking us to see some of the places where people go to be married.

First we go to the registry office. We meet Mrs Poole. She tells us that people don't need a ring to get married, but they do have to promise to love and look after each other.

We see the register where people sign their names when they marry.

At St Patrick's Church we meet Dave. He is the curate. He tells us how Christians get married in church. They make their special promises to each other and to God. Lydia and William will be married in a church.

When we go to the gurdwara, Mrs Bansal, our school secretary, comes with us. She is a Sikh, so she can explain what happens when Sikhs get married.

When we go in, we take off our shoes and cover our heads to show our respect. Mrs Bansal says that a Sikh bride and groom walk four times around the holy book, called the Granth Sahib. They make their promises to each other and to God. The giani (priest) lets us walk round the holy book.

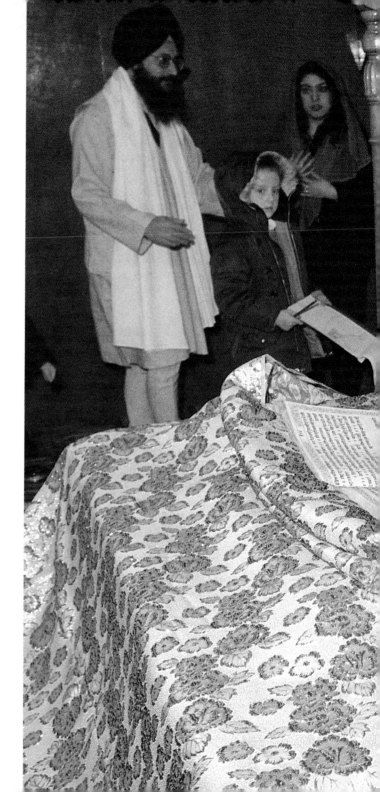

Today is Lydia's wedding day! I've been ready for ages when Tina comes to take me to the church.

Lydia and William belong to the same church, so they will be married there. The church has a very famous choir. I've seen Lydia and her friends singing on the television.

When we get to the church, I keep a look out for the wedding car.

Look what I see coming up the road.
It's a surprise from William's family. A horse
and carriage to take Lydia to the church.

In the church, Lydia and William make their promises to each other. They ask God to help them in their life together, and they promise to love and look after each other.

When the service is over, we have our photographs taken outside the church.
It's freezing! I'm glad when it's time to go to the reception at the town hall.

There are lots of people waiting for us. Lydia's mum puts Lydia's dress straight at the back so that she and William can lead us in. Everyone claps and cheers.

Pastor Basil stands up first.
He drinks a toast to Lydia and
William. They are Mr and Mrs Harris
now. He asks God to bless their
life together.

Then Lydia's mum and dad make
speeches. So does William's mum.
Lots of other people make speeches
to wish Lydia and William luck and
to ask God to bless them. Lydia and
William look very happy.

It's time to eat. There's curry and rice and lots more lovely food. I was too excited to eat breakfast, so I'm hungry. I even have a big piece of wedding cake.

Grandma and me think it's the best wedding ever.

Two weeks after the wedding, Lydia comes to school. We show her all the things we've made and she shows everyone the wedding photographs.

I look at the photographs with the other children. I can hardly believe that the bridesmaid is me.

More about the Evangelical Church

Lydia and William belong to the Evangelical Church. They are Christians who believe that Christ died on the Cross to make amends for all the bad things which people do. During an Evangelical Church service, people give thanks to God and ask for His help in their lives. The music during the service gradually changes from very slow to very fast and everyone claps, sings and joins in.

Sometimes, during the service, people talk about the things which have happened to them that week. If they are sad, they ask their friends and family to pray with them to help with their problems.

Things to do

1. Have you ever been to a wedding? Was it in a church, a gurdwara, a registry office, or somewhere else? Who helped with the wedding? A minister, an imam, a rabbi or someone else? What did people wear? Who came to the wedding? Did you have a special job to do? Tell the story and record it on a tape recorder. With your friends, you could make a collection of wedding stories.

2. Ask some of the older people you know if they have any photographs of their wedding. Look at the different clothes they wore.

At Christian weddings in this country, brides often wear white, but this has only been popular for about a hundred years. What were wedding clothes like before then? What colours do brides and grooms wear nowadays in weddings of other religions, or in other countries?

3. In South Wales, as the bride is leaving home she throws money to children. Can you find any other traditions for brides or grooms as they leave home? Ask your friends to help.

4. When people get married, we sometimes say they 'tie the knot'. At some weddings, 'tying the knot' is part of the ceremony. It shows how people will be tied together by marriage. A Hindu bridegroom knots a ribbon around his bride's neck. Do you know any other ways of 'tying the knot' at a wedding?

5. Lydia and William had music and singing at their wedding. Do you know any special songs for weddings?

6. Make your own word-search. Think of ten words to do with weddings; 'bride' could be one. Make a grid and put your ten words in different directions, either diagonal, horizontal or vertical.

Add any other letters to fill up the spaces in the grid. Give the word-search to a friend and ask him or her to find the words.

7. Do you know what confetti is? It is thrown over the bride and groom for luck. 'Confetti' is an Italian word. Do people in Italy throw confetti at weddings, or something else? In France, people throw sweets at a wedding, and in India they throw rice. Can you find out why?

Books to read

Jafta – The Wedding, *by Hugh Lewin and Lisa Kopper* (Dinosaur/Althea Books)
Wedding Day, *by Joan Solomon* (Hamish Hamilton)
Here Comes the Bride, *by Emil Pacholek* (Andre Deutsch)
A Sikh Wedding, *by Olivia Bennett* (Hamish Hamilton)